INVISIBLE THREADS

YEVGENY YEVTUSHENKO

INVISIBLE THREADS

DESIGNED BY CRAIG DODD

MACMILLAN PUBLISHING CO., INC.
NEW YORK

To Edward Steichen

Translated by Paul Falla and Natasha Ward

'Maternity Floor' translated by Arthur Boyars
'Safari in Ulster' translated by Ted Hughes
Excerpt from 'The Drunken Cow', from
The Face Behind the Mask,
translated by Arthur Boyars and Simon Franklin,
is included by permission of Marion Boyars Ltd

Macmillan Publishing Co., Inc.
866 Third Avenue, New York, N.Y. 10022

Library of Congress Cataloging in Publication Data
Yevtushenko, Yevgeny Aleksandrovich, 1933–
Invisible threads.

PG3476.E96A288 1981   891.71'44   81-8429
ISBN 0-02-632980-8   AACR2

10 9 8 7 6 5 4 3 2 1

Printed in Great Britain

CONTENTS

INVISIBLE THREADS

In every frontier-post
                there's something insecure.
Each one of them
                is mourning for the leaves and for the flowers.
They say
        the greatest punishment a tree can have
Is to become a frontier-post.
The birds that pause to rest
                on frontier-posts
Can't figure out
        what kind of tree they've landed on.
I suppose
        that at first, it was people invented frontiers,
And then the frontiers
                started inventing the people.
It was frontiers who invented
                customs-men and frontier-guards.
And frontiers who invented
            police,
               army,
                  and passports.
Thank God, though, we have
                invisible threads and threadlets,
Born of the threads of blood
                from the nails in the palms of Christ.
These threads struggle through,
                tearing apart the barbed-wire,
Leading love to join love,
                and anguish unite with anguish.
And a tear
        which evaporated somewhere in Paraguay
Will fall as a snowflake
                onto the cheek of an eskimo.
And a hulking New York skyscraper
That has forgotten the smell of the real earth, the smell of plough-lands,
Its brow lined with neon furrows,
Dreams only of embracing a tower from the Kremlin.
The Berlin Wall must think
'How much I would do, if I wasn't a frontier,
If laughing hands would pull me apart
To build funfairs,
           schools
              and hospitals.'
In dreams I see, like a damned ghost,
                my prehistoric ancestor;

He collected skulls, like trophies,
                              in the vaults of his sombre caves.
And with the bloodied tip of a stone spear
He marked out, on the face of the earth,
                              the first-ever frontier.
That was a hill of skulls.
                    Now it is grown an Everest,
The earth transformed,
                    become a giant burial-place.
While frontiers still stand
                    we are all still in prehistory.
Real history will start
                    when all the frontiers are gone.
The earth is all scarred,
                    mutilated with the scars of her wars.
Now killing has become an art
                    when once it was merely a trade.
In all those thousands of frontiers
                    the only one that we've lost is
                              the human one.
The frontier between good and evil.
But while we still have the invisible threads
Joining each 'self'
                    with millions of 'selves'
Then there is no separate
                    Ireland
                          or Haiti
Only humanity,
              a family (even if given to quarrels).
I am the echo of every voice in the world.
My soul has inhaled a million breaths.
I have in the world not one,
                    but millions of 'alter egos'.
Any man on this earth
                    is a super-power.
My government
              is the whole of humanity, all at once.
Every beggar is my marshal,
                    giving me my orders.
I am a racist,
              I recognize only one race –
The race of all races.
Nowhere
        am I a foreigner.
I have four-and-a-half billion leaders.
I dance my Russian – my mortally dangerous – dance
On the invisible threads
              that stretch between the hearts of men.

INTRODUCTION

The first time I was inspired by the muse of photography was in 1957 at the American Exhibition in Moscow. To be honest, a lot of Moscow's young people had gone along not to look at the exhibits but to taste the mysterious beverage known as Pepsi Cola. The satirical magazine *Krokodil* had always presented Coca Cola and Pepsi as capitalist poison – so why not try this mysterious poison that all America was drinking but never seemed to die of? Some lads went round in the queue so many times in the hope of feeling some effects, and became so bloated, that they had to be taken away in ambulances. It was there that I had my own first taste of Pepsi, and was disappointed; and there, too, with mixed feelings, that I first saw abstract paintings on show in Moscow.

But I also had another new experience. In due course I entered the crowded pavilion containing Edward Steichen's photographic composition *The Family of Man*; and when I came out I was a different person. All at once I had been swept clean of the Cold War's rubbishy propaganda, by the living breath of all humanity that issued from those photographs. I had never yet been in any country but my own – and now I felt I had simultaneously visited every nation of the world. It seemed to me that the exhibition was like a gigantic poem by Whitman, written not in words but with a camera. Through Steichen's photography, the invisible threads binding one nation to another had been made visible.

With me at that exhibition were some of my friends. We hardly spoke; we could only exchange looks. Yet somehow we expressed far more than we could have with any of the words of appreciation we failed to find. We were not to know then how widely we should come to be separated over the years. But the passage of time has still left intact the threads spun between us that particular day.

What kind of photography, though, had I known before this? Mostly, pictures of Stalin, of ceremonial meetings, of workers at their machines or of dairy maids standing beside cows with gold stars hanging round their necks. The faces in those photographs had either been masked by solemnity or else wore an official smile quite unlike anything in nature. In those days, I never thought of photography as art, but rather as something to do with official posters. As with many other writers, it was the cinema that had first brought about any change in me. When we were introduced to Italian films in the form of such works as *Rome, Open City* and *Bicycle Thieves*, it was a revelation. Previously we had been accustomed only to all those pompous films which ended with thousands of collective farmers banqueting in the open against a backdrop of power stations. But these new films had taught us to look further; for the first time we were shown that beauty can lie in the unbeautified. If I were to look for the origins of my own literary generation in Russia, I suspect I would find that we are all children of Italian neorealism – and not least because its influence brought us back to an appreciation of our own Russian realism.

Now, however, seeing Steichen's exhibition of photographs, we met with another order of revelation. It seemed that, like the cinema of Italian neorealism, it was a school in itself – but it was a school that revealed the world in terms we had never seen before. Through its depiction of humanity as one family, Steichen's photo-poem not only soared above the bickering of the Cold War. It also showed bonds of common feeling between nations that had been taught to fear each other. In his own way Steichen, through the sensitive use of camera and scissors to produce an anthology of sufferings and hopes, seemed to me Christ-like in his appreciation of all humanity. (Indeed, it can surely be only in such piecemeal ways that the hopes of Christianity will ever really take shape in this world.) Above all, the lesson taught by these photographs was that the ideal of human brotherhood can only be realized by the efforts of individuals to express it within themselves – and to do so by any means available. What difference whether it is through words, music, painting, cinema, photography or just everyday human actions that this ideal is made real? In these works of Steichen, the amorality or worse of inequality, exploitation, politicking, bureaucracy, racism and war was set against a vision of the world's essential beauty as knowable by all of us.

Some time later, I was actually able to meet Steichen, when together with a relative, the poet Carl Sandburg, he came to Moscow for an exhibition of his own. One's view of any nation as a whole can depend a lot on first contact with its individual citizens; and I was very lucky that the first Americans I ever met were both great men. Later, when in America itself I sometimes encountered dullards and rogues, it was always a great help to call to mind the faces of Steichen and Sandburg. I remembered Steichen's exhibition, too; and was able to remind myself that there is no such thing as a bad nation.

Photography, above all other arts, spins a web between one mind and another, and never more so than when overcoming the pain of loneliness.

For every human life is above all an attempt to overcome loneliness; to join the severed cord that once bound it with the rest of mankind. Inevitably, simply entering the world involves exchanging safety for rupture. The cutting of that cord banishes the security of the womb for ever, whether it is done by a surgeon's scissors in a hospital or by a peasant woman with her own teeth as she gives birth in the fields. Birth itself is the first breach of the thread binding the individual both to other people and to nature.

This was forcefully shown me when, in an English hospital, in Bournemouth, I was present at the birth of my own son. At first, when his head appeared out of his mother, I was terribly frightened – his eyes were closed; his body, as it followed, was a lifeless bluish colour; and indeed he looked as if he must be dead. The next moment, though, he opened his eyes, frowned, and began to cry, as if protesting at being separated from her. The doctor walked to the window without taking off his surgical gloves, groped for some cigarettes in the pocket of his white coat and promptly lit one. 'You're surprised to see him

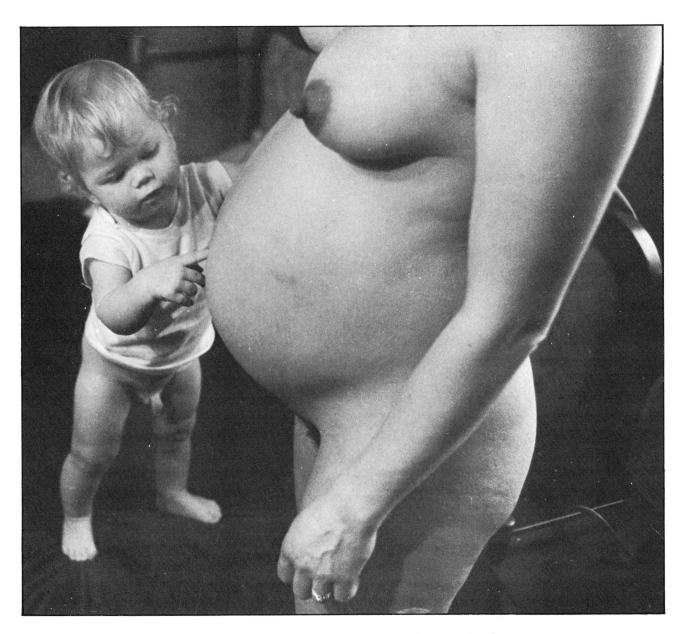

Ringing for His Baby Brother
(USSR)

Pressing his mother's tender navel – she is
Pregnant now with someone else –
The little boy in secret sounds a bell
To call his brother forth.
Press it and ring, to let the whole world
Hear your timid man-child's call.
And let us hope no grown-up will go mad
And sound the button to destroy us all.

looking so miserable? What do you expect? He has just come out of such a comfortable hotel, and found himself all alone in this huge uncomfortable world. He's feeling lonely . . .

But it was borne in upon me too that the loneliness of birth is felt by the mother as well as the child. Not for nothing do the English speak of a woman being in labour. She literally works with all her strength to deliver the child; and at this moment she is lonely as never before. One effect of the English idea of letting the man as well as the woman watch the miracle they have made together, is that it helps rescue the mother from her own isolation. The touch of her husband's hand in hers throughout the birth is a thread binding her, in a time of extremity, to the rest of humankind.

In modern times one form of division or dislocation within society is often blamed on ignoring the wisdom of our ancestors. What, after all, does the ordinary person know about his origins – his tribe? Most of us have never investigated any further back than our great grandparents. And how, asked the late nineteenth-century philosopher Nikolai Fyodorov, can one appreciate humanity as one family sprung from the same roots if almost none of us even knows the origins of his own individual family? Fyodorov himself believed humanity could overcome its divisions by uniting around one universal cause. The thing that makes us most aware of any shared cause is the sense of having an enemy in common. And all of us, he maintained, have such an enemy, regardless of religion, political creed or race – namely, death. No one, Zulu, Russian or Englishman, Moslem, Catholic or atheist, conservative or communist, wants to die. If, instead of spending huge sums on armies, weapons, police and bureaucracy, humanity would devote itself to fighting the common enemy then it might at least have some kind of victory to its credit. Perhaps, said Fyodorov, death was no more than a disease, a virus for which no antidote had yet been discovered. Long before the invention of the atom bomb, then, there were thinkers who already saw that humanity had only one choice: between universal brotherhood or universal destruction.

Yet today – need anyone ask which of these is more imminent? Existing stocks of nuclear weapons are enough to destroy every living thing several times over – yet still such weapons are being manufactured. Politics, instead of bringing people together, has set them against each other. Even if a new Christ were to answer our need and appear on earth, I fear there would still be people ready to use his message of unity as an instrument of chaos. Any political group who, having identified a true Messiah, could not appropriate him for itself would then simply declare him an agent of a hostile group. A new Christ would always find there were nails enough, ready to pierce his hands.

As a source of unity, patriotism is also suspect, according to Samuel Johnson. And with some all-important reservations I too would regard it as the last refuge of a scoundrel. Of course, if an individual American, Chinese or Russian could not justly love his country, it would make a mockery of all those other, personal ties that link humanity – the threads of feeling and even habit that join parent and child or connect the living with their own forebears. But patriotism misdirected to serve the selfishness of nations as a whole is a scourge. In its place, there can only be a patriotism of people, of the whole human race.

Humankind is the common body of us all; and all human beings are its mysteriously connected organs, arteries, veins, capillaries and cells. The left hand should never gloat when the right hand is injured. Sometimes, though, when you read the newspapers or listen to the radio, the excitement with which they describe troubles or even tragedies in other countries can only move you to astonishment. How can any man cure himself by using the sickness of another as his own medicine? Occasionally, when I hear one government hypocritically denouncing another, I am reminded of an old prostitute with incurable syphilis triumphantly accusing a younger member of the profession of having gonor-rhoea. (Forgive the crudity of my comparison, but one cannot write about national interests without also passing some such metaphorical judgement on the old and unclean profession of politics.)

Whatever the danger of falling, politically speaking, between two stools, maybe we should be prepared to suffer any pains if this will save us from petty-minded factionalism. Christ disdained the standpoint both of the Pharisees and of Pontius Pilate – even though the middle ground between them proved to be the cross. But from his nailed hands invisible links have reached out to all humankind. Not the canny puppet-strings with which tyrants and other aggressors practise their manipulations, but threads binding us to the awareness of a condition higher than mere freedom; to a consciousness of Christ's own hallowed un-freedom from the sufferings of all humanity.

Since that day at the American Exhibition in 1957, when photography's potential as an international language first burst upon me so dramatically, I have travelled in sixty-four countries. The experience has done nothing to dissuade me from a belief that the workings of the human heart are the same under any political system. I believe that natural good rules the hearts of most people in this world, but that political organization allows a few men to warp the minds of this majority. In their hands the mass media have become a paper curtain no less impenetrable than one of iron, hiding the essential humanity of those who live out of sight beyond the curtain. The power of those who corrupt us depends on maintaining the lie that behind the curtain the only creatures to be found are utter aliens. But on both sides of this barrier people laugh, cry, love, suffer, long for happiness – and create the stuff of true art – in exactly the same way.

Of all the artistic drives, perhaps the strongest is the happiness to be had from successful self-expression. Obviously, only total idiots can be totally happy. For the rest of us, the knowledge of suffering, even learned from a distance, ought to make moral anaesthesia a crime. But if indifference to other people's well-being is an unpardonable offence, we do have the right to seek at least some form of happiness for ourselves.

And what is human happiness? Surely it is to fulfil oneself, by the use of every gift that nature has bestowed. Of course there is a darker side to the exercise of some talents. Tyranny itself, in the shape of bureaucracy, is an art form of a kind. Yet in return for the satisfaction it can give, through the knowledge of a job efficiently done, it lays waste its subjects' lives twice over. Having thwarted their pursuit of happiness it annihilates even their desire to be happy, since ultimately it seeks to hinder the enjoyment of any creative act whatever.

Can bureaucracy itself show a talent for anything but the perverted art of obstructing other people's lives? Certainly individual bureaucrats, no less than Newton, Einstein, Mozart, Rembrandt, Tolstoy, have been great men in their mothers' wombs. But bureaucracy can kill off talent even in its own practitioners. Seeing their own gifts as a liability, they can only respond to other people's talents by assassinating these as well. Bureaucracy is indifference transformed into an act of aggression. It may not wallop people's heads off with the violence of an old-time tyrant; but with its own tidy precision it leaves them amputated for all that.

And indifference is a disease, as surely as if we could inhale it in the form of microbe-infested air. Yet the vaccines do exist that can hold off this affliction. Not the least of them is an awareness of man-made beauty – which in turn depends on a feeling for nature. A quarter of the world's population, diverted by hunger and blocked by ignorance, has no notion of its own kind's highest artistic achievements. But even where knowledge of El Greco, Shakespeare or Dostoyevsky has been denied, say, to a Kampuchean or an Eskimo, there is another, equal satisfaction that cannot be stolen from him. One might describe it as the art of nature. Even in the teeth of deprivation and distress, people persist in seeking happiness such as we can gain from contemplating great works of art, by opening themselves instead to a knowledge of nature, the fountainhead of man's artistic endeavours. In so doing, men and women who have never studied at any art school are moved to take part in miracles of their own making, to add to the world's sum of beauty and compete with nature as an act of worship, by carving on rocks, making sculptures or devising songs. Every religion on earth has been conceived by this yearning for beauty and delivered into the world by artists; and despite the combined desecrations of bureaucrats and clerics, every religion has a beauty of its own.

The art that has created all religions is itself a religion; for art teaches us not only a sense of beauty but also an awareness of good and evil. And yet the indivisibility in art between ethics and aesthetics is today challenged more strenuously than ever before. The struggle extends through every form of art. At issue is whether art in fact comprises a religion in its own right or is merely a minion of commerce.

In modern times this strife has come to include in its recruits the newer muses born of technical progress: those of the cinema and photography. Against the muse of the cinema, to whom we owe *The Battleship Potemkin, City Lights, Citizen Kane, 8½, 1900, One Flew Over The Cuckoo's Nest, Ashes and Diamonds* and *Andrei Rublyov*, there are ranged not only films of pornography, violence, and shallow unfelt comedy, but television in all its more dispiriting forms.

The muse of the photographic art is perhaps even more embattled, confronted as she is by the anti-muse of commercial photography, which is in the pay of the advertisers of bras, braces, liquor, sun beaches, airlines and motor cars. On the middle ground, meanwhile, documentary photography performs a useful service; though for the most part it finds itself as far removed from the muse of photography as political commentaries are from great poetry. Then there is private photography, which has an ambiguous and highly varied role to play. At its most trivial it offers nothing more than the illusion – albeit a pleasant one – of being involved in an actual art, as you click away at members of the family or make a private record of a holiday resort. But in fairness it should be said that many amateurs are gifted enough to go far beyond the bounds of dilettantism. They have it in them to become captivated, through their view-finder, by a world quite different from the one they see only with the naked eye; and their attempts to capture what they see often show the freshness and exuberance of a great primitive work of art. Their very amateurism is thus turned into creative achievement, and in this way the muse of photography lays its hand in blessing on accountants, chemists, fitters and geologists who never for a moment suspected they might become great artists. And even to be such a thing during the blink of a shutter is a prodigious achievement; for it is in this instant that one can make visible the thread binding us to the rest of humanity.

But why did I myself take up photography?

As a poet, I always found it went against the grain just to write for a small number of cognoscenti. From the start I wanted my verses to appeal to people who do not usually read poetry; and in my own country – and to some extent in others too – I hope I have since achieved this. But once translated, the language of poetry becomes fragile and exposed. It is like touching a butterfly's wings – rough handling destroys the colour for ever. Experience of this with my own work has made me desperately jealous of artists such as composers and painters, since their language needs no translation. But I am not good at music or painting; so for me there remained one language – photography.

I have always been rather overawed by technology, so I began with the easiest camera of all, the Polaroid. What tempted me was the possibility of not having to bother with developing and printing. But the Polaroid was a disappointment. It is all right for family snapshots; but nothing more. I might have stopped taking photographs altogether – but for the example I gained through actually meeting some true artist photographers.

When I first came into the public eye, I soon found myself surrounded by the clicking of other people's cameras. In time, though, I realized that by comparison with what these were producing, the click of the art photographer's camera represents something quite different. I got to know and like such people as Seeliger from *Stern*, Marc Riboud, Rene Burri and Elliot Erwitt of *Magnum*, and Newman of *Life*; and during our time together on tour we became firm friends and I learned greatly to respect their profession. In London in 1961 I met and became friends with William Klein, who presented me with a copy of his beautiful book on Paris. Subsequently he produced two fine works on Tokyo and Moscow; and I think it was these books which gave me the urge to take up serious photography. One particular thing about them that still amazes me is that Klein shows no interest in having his pictures in focus; also his unfocused machine-gun shots are unusually dynamic – everything in them seems to move.

In addition to being impressed by Klein's technique, I was particularly struck by the fact that he, a foreigner, in a few days had managed to see Russia in a way that I as a Russian had never done. Cartier-Bresson's Russian photographs affected me in the same way. I even felt aggrieved that some aspects of the life of my country which I had never noticed had been revealed instead by foreigners. It had never occurred to me that in real art there are no aliens. Later I came to

Self-portrait
(USSR)

All our strength is spent ascending
Ladders into the unknown
But there's always one last rung, and
One inviolable law:
If you climb the ladder higher
Then your fall will hurt the more.
And perhaps we don't need ladders
If we want to reach the sky;
Maybe, ladderless, deservers
Get a stern but kindly hand.

A social climber (self-portrait taken by automatic)

Curiosity
(Australia)

Curiosity one may observe
Even at the zoo, in a giraffe
Victimized by others' stares.
Thank God its neck is long enough at least
To overtop the limits of its pen
And gulp at least a snatch of liberty
And get one lick of freedom from the sky.
But how can any man outside the cage,
Seeing the giraffe, not envy him?
His neck is shorter than the beast's,
His own life, shorter still.

17

see, as part of the truths I attempted to voice in 'Suffering cannot be foreign', that art, too, cannot be foreign, simply because compassion – the sharing of suffering – is one of its essentials.

The first person to put a real camera into my hands was Rene Burri, while we were both present at an African tribal festival. I tried very hard to make the best of my attempts; and when the results were printed Burri sent them on to me himself, saying, to my incredulity, that they did actually show signs of ability. Later, in 1973, during a trip to Japan, I was accompanied by a number of professional Japanese photographers, and it was they who persuaded me finally to buy a camera, a Nikon F that I have to this day. After that, I armed myself with a few lenses, which were bulky but indispensable. I discovered what any photographer needs is a strong neck, so that he can carry several cameras at once, loaded with different films – both colour and black-and-white – and a bag of lenses.

But a camel can carry a lot more hardware than a man and still not take photographs. Two things in particular are essential to the art of photography: constant readiness, and selection. The law of ill-luck dictates that the best pictures always turn up when you don't actually have your camera with you. And when you have, they refuse to materialize. You have to keep your camera at the ready all the time and not overload yourself with lenses. I, for instance, find that three are quite enough: 52mm, 20mm and a 200mm zoom. I'm also fond of using the wide-angle. It enhances the depth, and in close up it gives the rather attractive effect of a slight distortion; in the human body, for example, this produces the elongated appearance of a painting by El Greco.

With a few exceptions I don't like framing. If the picture I see framed in the view-finder appears worth taking in the first place, it should be capable of making a complete composition in its own right. Ideally, selection should happen right at the outset, in the act of shooting, with a combination of instinct and calculation to tell you at once whether any particular picture is worth taking.

No one, though, can avoid taking bad pictures. It was while using the first camera I ever owned that I came to appreciate one of the iron rules of photographic art. Just as it may need several rough drafts to complete a poem properly, to take one good photograph you may have to spoil quite a lot of film. So, after shooting, there usually does have to come the second selection: the assessment of the developed film. Which frames are worth printing after all? One day I had been out taking pictures near a Moscow railway station. In my mind had been the theme of heaviness – people overloaded beneath their bags and bundles. Afterwards, as I started looking through the contact prints, I gasped; there in front of a peasant woman weighed down with bundles was an enormous Brocken-like shadow. At the instant of shooting I hadn't noticed that shadow. But it was this that made the photograph. 'Some idiots are lucky,' I said to the lab assistant. He shook his head. 'You didn't spot the shadow when you were shooting,' he replied. 'But you did spot it on a tiny contact print and saw at once what it would do when enlarged. You're not such an idiot; you do know a thing or two.'

Technically, though, I'm still a photographic ignoramus. I don't develop and I don't print; I haven't the time – or perhaps I just lack the ability. Let me tell the story of the day when, after three exhibitions and quite a few articles about me as a photographer, I showed my total ignorance. Someone from a newspaper had phoned to ask me for a few sheets of Kodak photographic paper. In broad daylight on a sunny day I calmly unsealed a large packet of Kodak, took out the required sheets and set off with them to his office. This caused a great deal of laughter, and I failed to understand what it was all about. I hadn't even known that photographic paper was sensitive to light. (And I could kick myself, too, for all the times my films are over- or under-exposed.) Likewise one day in Leningrad, having taken thirty-six shots, I came home feeling overjoyed at having taken some brilliant pictures – only to find I'd been using an unloaded camera.

But nothing in art is completely wasted – not even failure. I always retain some image, even of the pictures that don't come out, because their subject is, I know, something I have recorded not only with my camera but also with my soul. There are faces whose image I have never succeeded in transferring onto film but which for all that have gone on living inside me, to the point where they have become my own face. In photography the absence of indifference is all. What some experts call 'the objective' – the lens – should really be nothing of the kind. It may be loving, tender, sarcastic, mocking, suffering, aggressive – all or any of these rather than merely dispassionate. It was Steichen's exhibition that taught me this and for this reason it is to him that I respectfully dedicate my first book of photographs. Confronted by that philosophy of invisible threads embodied for me by his *Family of Man*, I see myself merely as a disciple. But at the risk of exaggerating my own abilities, I am not prepared to underestimate that discipleship. The object of my poems and photographs is precisely to prevent any snapping of those links between different people. And even if they have been broken in the past, I can become a knot, small but strong, joining them together once more.

In a sense my career as a photographer has lasted all my life – although it has not always been pursued through the use of a camera. I have an excellent visual memory, and from childhood on I learned to take photographs, as it were, with my eyes. One day during the war I was standing on a platform singing songs in return for bread. A peasant woman, who had been listening to me with tears in her eyes, took out a piece of bread wrapped in a cloth. Carefully, so as not to lose a crumb, she broke it in two, gave me half, and asked me to sing something more. I did so; she then broke her half in two again and gave me half. I remember that woman's face down to the last wrinkle, as if I had photographed it not only with my eyes but with my heart.

Had I been a painter I doubt I should have produced either abstracts or landscapes, though I feel no particular antipathy towards abstract art, and have a great love of nature. I feel sure I would have painted the human face. For I feel nothing on earth is more capable of fascinating; it is an aspect of creation that moves me to ask, in the words of Dostoyevsky, 'Is there anything more fantastic than reality?'

For a poet, the basis of his work is of course the testimony of his own inner world. But the majority of people neither write poetry nor immortalize their private selves in any other way. Their thoughts and feelings disappear with

A Triangle
(USSR)

Albert Todd, my American friend,
Professor at Queen's College, in New York,
A handsome grey man, with a limp,
Looking like a wolf with many wounds,
Once, feeling tired, supine upon the grass,
Crossing his legs, had made a shape,
A triangle in which, far off,
A little girl sat, pensive, like
An ancient dame, her elbow on her knee.

My friend, forgive my cruelty –
In private, still, you think you're young.
Exactly so I see myself, and yet
Eternal youth is nowhere on this earth,
And no way can a girl, today a child,
In ten years' time, say, care for you or me.
For her each one of us will be too old;
And yet our tragedy is not in this,
But in the fact this flusters us.
And yet, you know, how foolish are our fears!
Though no one cares to know he's old
It's just this knowledge that can make him young.

them when they die. So art is perhaps our only successful attempt at the conquest of death. The poems of my own that I value most are those in which it is not I who speak, so much as other people through me; the poems in which I become their voice and thus help save them from the prospect of extinction after their lives are done. This it is – the capacity to speak through another person – that since my childhood has particularly endeared the ballad form to me, as exemplified, say, by Kipling in masterpieces of poetic photography like *The Mary Gloster*. To achieve this effect, though, one must not only listen to people but be able to photograph them with one's heart. Not just poetry, but prose works too, may fail if their creator lacks the ability to project other people's images onto himself in this way. In Dostoyevsky's work for example the characters are nothing but great metaphorical photographs.

In trying to give a faithful likeness of someone in words rather than an actual photograph, one invaluable gift is the ability to hold in the mind's eye a whole mass of separate images. In this way one can both reveal the universal in an individual, and vice versa. I once read my long – 4,000-line – poem about the workers of the Bratsk power station in Siberia to the workers themselves. There were about two thousand of them in the hall, many of them straight from the site and still wearing their overalls because there had been no time to change. At any big construction site there are always a lot of unmarried mothers and they too came to my reading, all spattered with cement and whitewash. They couldn't leave their children at home, so they brought them along as well. One section of the poem took the form of a monologue by one such woman. When I finished reading that part, all over the hall as if by some magic inaudible signal these women stood up and lifted their children in their arms as much as to say, 'Here we are . . . Yes, we know you were writing about us.'

No prize could compare with their response. It was the finest piece of recognition I have ever been awarded. I had not written specifically about any of those women, even though each of them thought that section was about herself. But to create just one metaphorical likeness, I had had to photograph dozens of them with my eyes and heart. And they were right – I had meant to write about each one of them.

In such ways as this have I embraced both muses – of poetry and of photography. I came to the latter – 'the omnipotent god of detail', to use Pasternak's expression – because on my pages I wanted to replace poetic representations of people's faces with the faces themselves. I have always been more moved by the human face than by any other influence on earth; and I know of nothing more astonishing, more diverse, more original and more precious. To me it is an unsurpassable witness to the beauty of the unbeautiful, the generosity of the destitute, the pride of the humiliated and the inborn strength of the defenceless.

But whatever private qualities individual people may have, most of them go unremarked by anyone. Millions live without the slightest hope of being known to posterity. When they die, their faces vanish with them. The worst of this is that each face is both a cache of unique secrets and, potentially, an historical record. In the past it might have been made accessible to us only via portraiture – but there were not enough artists to go round. Gioconda and Saskia were lucky, for these wonderful women would have vanished into oblivion had it not chanced that each was favoured by a genius. Now, across the centuries, their smiles survive to weave invisible threads between their lives and ours.

There have been millions of others, though, whose faces, without photography, would never have been recorded. Not a single witness would have observed the whole separate world that existed behind each of those faces.

Let us take an individual example from real life. A tired ageing woman encumbered with baggage trudges across Moscow. The weight of everyday life has left her face almost without any sign of character. She has already forgotten when it was last admired – if indeed it ever was. This woman has never been famous in her own country, much less worldwide. Her appearance is universal for all that, in that her shoulders bear the burdens of every working mother that ever was. But she has never been drawn, because she has never known an artist; and if she has ever been photographed, it has only been for her passport or some other official form.

Suddenly her way is barred. A rope is stretched across the pavement and a group of little girls, squealing with glee, are skipping. Instead of getting cross, the woman puts down her bags and stands watching them; and as she does so her face gradually kindles with the recollection of how she too used to skip merrily over the rainbow of a twirling rope. Her expression changes once more, showing in the same instant both the sorrow of the gone-forever and the joy of knowing that life, regardless of her own waning existence, goes on. But who, perceiving these emotions, can capture them? Only a photographer.

Photography, then, is a form of confession; it is a rescue from oblivion; it voices the silent monologues of those who cannot express themselves through literature. It is a film in which all the cast are stars; it is the music of life stopped for an instant; and as motionless television it enables nobodies to be observed by celebrities.

Yet people often do not like being photographed; and when they do face a camera they usually prefer to be well-dressed and smiling. If they overhear the click of the shutter in moments of exhaustion, sadness or despair, they are as likely as not to think their picture is being taken in order to mock them. They do not realize the extent to which the camera is their advocate. For example I don't like taking pictures of women who are commonly considered beautiful. My beauties are old women – even though they are often shy, and afraid of their wrinkles.

On one occasion, in the red-light district of Sydney, in pursuit of one of my favourite themes – heaviness – I was busy taking a picture of a huge man laden with all sorts of things. He was pushing a pram full of books, dishes and other odds and ends; and to cap it all, on his back he was carrying a refrigerator. As I was aiming my camera I suddenly felt a sharp blow on my cheek. I lowered the camera and found myself looking at a prostitute. The blow had come from an empty Pepsi Cola bottle. The prostitute was about to take a swipe at my camera, too; but at the last moment – out of respect for property over persons? – she was considerate enough to leave only a small mark on the edge of the lens (I still regard it as an honourable scar). She was feeling insulted, under the illusion that I had been trying to photograph *her*.

There have been other, similar misunderstandings. There was one incident when at a market in Hong Kong some old Chinese women pelted me with rotten potatoes. And once in my home country, at Zima Junction in Siberia, some workers I'd photographed drinking beer at a stall grabbed me and marched me off to the local administration as an American spy. When this misunderstanding had been cleared up, one of them said, 'Is that the way to take photographs? We were in our work clothes, not properly shaved, and holding beer mugs . . . You ought to have warned us and we'd have smartened ourselves up. Then you could have taken all the pictures you liked.'

Any number of the people I have tried to record on film may have failed to understand even the least part of my purpose. And few indeed may have known the full truth: that I was trying to create invisible links between them, reminding the world at large of their own separate, unrenowned yet unique and precious existences.

In this book there are hardly any famous people. But I hope the people in it will become famous for those who turn these pages. And if any of you, who read this book, take into your hearts for ever the face of a Russian granny or an old man from Svanetia or a Filipino boy, or the silhouette of a Canadian boy and girl holding each other close under the flags of all the nations of the world, I shall be happy to think that through me an invisible thread has become interwoven in those flags.

Yevgeny Yevtushenko
Peredelkino, 31 March 1980

LIFE AND DEATH

One day, Death came complaining to Life:
'They hate me, all of them, and fear me.
Let's change places for a while,
Even if it's only for a week.
I'll be Life. And you'll turn into Death.'
Death wondered a bit at the way that Life
Agreed without giving it a moment's thought,
Covered her face at once with the skull-mask,
Hiding her hundred freckles beneath the skull,
Took up the scythe, testing it with her finger,
And smiling in satisfaction when she saw
The spot of blood it left upon her finger;
She strode away,
Her eyes laughing out of the holes in the skull,
And shouted happily from afar:
'Remember, it was your idea!'
Death turned into Life. She slid a skin
Over her skeleton. On came the jeans,
The T-shirt on which John Travolta bared his teeth.
She stuck on a nose, then powdered it,
Used her influence to get hold of the hundred freckles
(Although, if you counted them carefully, you would find
Not more than ninety-nine.
The most important one was missing).
To cover up the smell of grave
Death gave an international dab –
'Chanel' from Paris onto one cheek,
'Red Moscow' on the other;
And oiling her bones with the finest English baby-cream
To stop them rattling
She set off, swaying at the hips.
Death, modestly decked out as life,
Passed through the walls, into the Kremlin and White House;
She went into the House of Commons
And democratically took her place in the queue
For the Ladies, behind Mrs Thatcher.
And Death breathed the smoke of press-conferences,
And witnessed pre-election speeches,
And, most important, she listened to the millions
Who will never be elected to anything.
Death went into the slums of Manila,
And saw a child, new as misfortune.
Where 'life' means 'hunger',
And brings no cause for joy.

Nobody smiled back at Death
When she smiled, all dressed as Life,
At the mournful Londonderry children
And the forgotten Kampuchean refugees,
Heaped up like piles of cod, in boats.
No longer was their feeling hate for life;
They were already filled with indifference.
The week passed, and they met again.
Death, acting Life, looked just like death,
Angry, exhausted and sick.
Life, acting Death, looked just like life,
Young, and all blossoming.
Said Death: 'Well, now I understand
Your cunning when you acquiesced.
Before, although I was always feared, I was also respected.
Death is respected, but never Life.
You know what a frightening thing I learned?
That a disrespect for Life is the life of all those
Who do not respect themselves
(Although all their self-esteem
Is stamped upon their faces, like a seal).
What respect is there for life, where people
Waste their only life upon
Their own meanness, clothes and money,
Their thirst for power that's gained by murder?
How many of them defile their own lives,
Then spit and grouse: ''Life? You call this life?''
When I was Death, although they feared me
They strewed me with flowers.
I kept so many people in work,
Making me in bombs
And oral contraceptives.
And now what has become of me?
Now that I'm life, I cannot give them work.
Although I suffered, by being Death
I brought relief to many,
Hope in another, different life,
A life (as I well know) not to be found,
But if your life is hopeless, death means hope.
That's what keeps all the religions going.
And even if the sight of death makes people cry,
At least they do not curse it.
When I turned into Life, the whole earth
Called me ''accursed'' . . .'
Sighed Death: 'How terrible to be Life.'
Sighed Life: 'How marvellous to be Death.'
And suddenly they wept, and they embraced,
And there was suddenly no telling Life from Death.

SALVATION

Our salvation is in one another,
In the divinely closed circle,
With no way in for outsiders,
Where the only third party is Nature.

Our salvation is in one another
In the snowstorm we break into two,
In the sunshine we break into two.
Equal halves. That's our salvation.

Our salvation is in one another.
In the sudden fear that grips the heart
That we might be forever apart
And fall into the hands of another.

Our parents can never defend us.
We are children of one another – no one else.
We'll have to bring ourselves up.
We ourselves are our parents.

What false passions
For money and power.
The only true passion
Is of two, united for ever.

World fame is but a phantom
If the woman you love ignores you.
I wish I was forgotten by others,
And famous only for you!

Ever pouring from one to the other,
We are fused. Like stalactites,
The Northern Lights –
Are they not our conjunction?

Ninety per cent of the people
Have never known real love.
That is why they are so narrow,
The apostles of power and anger.

But if among the eunuchs
Even two lovers are left
Then we can hope in truth,
For humanity is still alive.

All life stands on love.
Two – that's a great army
Murmuring, lips and hands:
'Our salvation is in one another.'

THE SMILE

When the eunuchs of these latter days
Condemn whoever fails to share their gods,
From pagan times
Truly an ancient priesthood finds its voice.

Stupid people hold it their delight
To make a butt of unstupidity;
But how, if being faithful to yourself,
Smiling, you thwart them even in their sleep!

Whenever the game
Is 'heads or tails'
The side that lands face up's
The one that smiles.

The murderer, perceiving his monstrosity,
Will tremble at himself, and
At the knowledge of superiority
Seen in the ruin of the corpse's mouth.

Even so the slave, downtrodden,
Gave the priest a sudden smile so far from humble
That it collapsed – which empire?
– Hammurabi's, shall we say?

27

THE LAST FAITH

Are we really all so deformed
That for us there is no salvation?
Are ideas really grounded, now,
In the age when man flies in space?

Will the last crooked birch
Bending over the last river
See the last human being
In its boiling waters?

Will there really be no more Big Ben,
Empire State, Kremlin, Notre Dame,
Will our last footsteps be effaced
Beneath a stream of bubbling lava?

That the planet should perish
The blossoms, the birds and the children,
I can't believe . . .
          I suppose this
Is my last faith.
The last soldier on earth
Will fling his epaulettes into the stream
And smile placidly
As the dragonflies use them for a perch.
All villainy will end
All men will understand that we are a family.
The last government
Will abolish itself.
The last exploiter
Will open his toothless mouth,
And glancing warily over his shoulder,
Swallow the last money, like a last tasty morsel.
And the last censor
Will be condemned, for life,
To recite (with expression) on stage
All that he ever cut out.

And the last bureaucrat
(To give him some quiet and rest)
Will have the last rubber stamp in the world
Rammed home into his throat.

And the earth will turn on its axis
Without the terror of recent years.
And never will we see the birth
Of the last of the world's great poets . . .

At the rustle of a field of clover
At the creak of the pines in the wind
I stand still, and listen, and remember
That I, too, will die one day.

A boy appears on the roof
By a drain-pipe, with a taut pigeon
I see that it's cruel to die
Cruel to oneself – and, even more, to others.

You can't feel life unless you can feel death.
We don't just flow away, like water into sand.
But the living – those who take the place of the dead –
Could never replace them . . .

I've seen a few things about life,
So I didn't get my beatings for nothing.
I think I've forgotten all that I remembered,
But remember all that I forgot.

I've seen that snow is softer in childhood
The hills are greener when you're young.
I've seen that life is many lives
If in your life you've had many loves.

I've seen that I was in mysterious communion
With so many people, all from different times.
I've seen that what makes men unhappy
Is that endless search for happiness . . .

Sometimes happiness is oh, so thick and stupid
The gaze of happiness is empty and shallow.
Grief, when it looks, it strains and trembles
And that is why its stare pierces so deeply . . .

Happiness is a glance from an aeroplane window;
Grief sees the earth unadorned.
In happiness there is a certain treachery;
Grief will never betray.

I was mindlessly happy in my time.
Thank God, nothing came of it.
I wanted the impossible.
Luckily, I didn't get it.

I love you, my fellow-men,
And forgive you your pursuit of happiness.

RESURRECTION

Our resurrection is in one another;
Not in some distant heaven, but ourselves.
And if heaven absolutely must exist,
Then let it show itself in each of us.

If to confess our sins we go to church
Why shouldn't we then go among ourselves
To make our dearest confidence,
To every man each other soul a church?

When we say God is somewhere up above,
We lose the deity that lives in every man.
When murder practises hypocrisy upon its knees
How hard it seeks a God who lacks a human face.
Make me a part of God, but God as man!

It's dignity that counts
Since anyway the times,
Stagnant or turbulent,
Must be endured.

It's dignity that counts.
Or else the dolers-out of charity
Will lead you mangerwards to
Stop your mouth with hay.

Perhaps you'll be forgotten by your son,
Those near to you extinguished, every one;
Perhaps not love alone but even what
You only thought was love, will cease.

And what if, waking, helplessly you find
A sodden stupor's lasted you the war,
And you yourself are naked and alone
Upon the bare inglorious earth?

But even then, when, past the power
Of foresight to perceive, failure's the rule,
Acknowledge to yourself this simple truth:
'This too had to be endured.'

THE CROOKED MOTOR

Free from care and spoiling for a lark,
We zigzag down the River Vilyuy,
Tanked up twice over, ragamuffins all,
From choice in keen pursuit of roughing it.
Six layabouts of forty years apiece,
Both our boats devoid of any angler's catch.
The duralumin boat becomes a pie
Whose filling is the gap our girls have left.
Our jostled livers live like refugees in the inflatable.
The shingle's kisses nearly wrench the engine off.
Diving-birds, upon their perches, preen themselves;
The engine, like a drunkard's morning-after mouth, hangs all askew.
The spoon-bait, smitten by the rocks, has grown a kink,
The knock-kneed oar is bent.
Scraggy-throated, all the cliffs –
Likewise our crumpled cigarettes – are out of shape.
Yet even while our nerves are plucked as if they made an instrument,
Somehow our crooked course propels us on
Towards a prospect fraught with destiny. And,
Mis-shapen as it may be, there's our engine.
It may be out of shape, but still it goes.
And only pseuds declare themselves for driving straight.
How can your course be straight in any case
If even your technology is all to hell?
The wrong benzine shoves us on our way,
Our rubber boat is patched,
The stench of fuel has our senses in revolt
And our very hearts propel us crookedly.
Of course a straight line was the form we meant our lives to take,
However tortuous they've come to be.
Charybdis, I never flinched aside from you,
But still my face got bashed in by an underwater rock.
Come to that, Scylla, I've not sidestepped you,
And yet you too have left me all awry.
It's not as if I've started practising timidity;
My smile, for all that, grows lopsided,
My love, half-dead, distorted
Like a sapling that's been waterlogged.
Onlookers innocent of wet or cold
Use opera glasses to examine me
Patching the boat with fragments of my hide.
But what the hell!
   Gosha, pull that rope!

Our motor may be crooked, and our course;
But our fate's curving path propels us up
To orbit who knows where,
And – who knows – the very rivers of the underworld
May straighten us, for all eternity.
Spectators, cavilling, leave me unmoved.
I am one of those who shot the rapids
With a crooked motor, but a real one,
On a real course, fatal though it be.

A Pregnant Man

Now here's an oddity; behold, a pregnant man.
An alien burden makes me totter and devours my strength,
As if I bore the world itself in embryo,
Not merely for a term but all eternity,
As if with millions of feet it pummelled my insides.
Within my belly every pregnant woman grows apace
And, simultaneously, every child.
Among my foetuses there number bombs and tanks,
Kisses, flowers and putrefying bones.
Time and again I suffer stabbing from within,
Pierced by the Kremlin battlements and Eiffel Tower;
Within me are the oceans surging to and fro,
America and Russia too, like Siamese twins.
My eyes are pregnant with the faces of mankind,
My ears with bird-song heard at break of day.
My heart is pregnant with all hearts,
And every wise man grows to fulness in my head.
(If only that could spare me from stupidity!)
But what fate is there worse than carrying a rogue!
I dreamed the makings of all killers,
Bureaucrats, police and armies could be shed –
For what fate could surpass aborting those!
I'm pregnant with all tears and laughter on this earth.
And having quietly infiltrated my own womb, I bear myself.
I carry every mortal whose conception is to come,
And all who, having died, are yet to rise.

I WOULD LIKE

I would like to be born in every country
Have a passport for them all to throw the foreign office into a panic.
Be every fish in every ocean
and Every dog in the streets of the world,
I would rather be a dog among dogs
than in a foreign country a wog among wogs.

I don't want to bow down before any idols
Or play at being a Russian Orthodox church hippy,
But I would like to plunge deep into Lake Baikal
and surface snorting somewhere – why not in the Mississippi?

In my damn beloved universe
I would like to be a lonely weed,
But not a delicate pansy – in both meanings.
I would like to be any of God's creatures
Right down to the last mangy hyena –
But never a tyrant or even the cat of a tyrant.
I would like to be reincarnated as a man –
In any image:
– a victim of prison torture
– a homeless child in the slums of Hong Kong
– a living skeleton in Bangladesh,
– a holy beggar in Tibet
– a black in Cape Town,
but never in the image of a bastard.

I would like to lie under the knives of all the surgeons in the world:
Hunchbacked, blind –
Suffer all kinds of diseases, wounds and scars,
be a victim of war,
Or a sweeper of dog-ends,
Just so a filthy microbe of superiority doesn't creep inside.
I would not like to be in the élite,
Nor, of course, in the cowardly herd,
Nor a guard-dog of that herd,
Nor a shepherd, sheltered by that herd,
and I would like happiness,
But not at the expense of the unhappy –
and I would like freedom,
But not at the expense of the unfree.
I would like to love all the women in the world,
And I would like to be a woman, too –
                              just once . . . . . .

Men have been diminished by Mother Nature.
Why won't you give motherhood to men?
If an innocent child stirred below his heart,
Men would probably not be so cruel.
I would like to be man's daily bread – say –
A cup of rice for a Vietnamese woman in mourning
or an onion in the slops of a prison
– cheap wine in a Neapolitan workers' trattoria
Or a tiny tube of cheese in orbit round the moon:
let them eat me;
Let them drink me –
If my death will be of some use.

I would like to belong to all times –
Shock all history so much
That it was amazed what a smart Alec I was
– saw up Stenka Razin's wooden cage,
– save Mary Stuart's fragile neck from that impolite axe,
– bring Nefertiti to Pushkin on a troika.
I would like to increase the space of a moment a hundredfold,
So that in that same moment
I could drink vodka with fishermen in Siberia,
Kiss in Liverpool, whispering Liverpudlian,
And sit together with Homer, Dante, Shakespeare, and Tolstoy drinking
Anything, except of course, Coca Cola.
– dance to the tom toms in the Congo,
– strike at Renault,
– chase a ball with Brazilian boys at Copacabana Beach.
I would like to know every language,
Like the secret waters under the earth,
And do all kinds of work at once.
I would make sure that one Yevtushenko was merely a poet.
The second an underground fighter, somewhere,
the third – a student at Berkeley,
the fourth – a jolly Georgian drinker,
And the fifth maybe a teacher of Eskimo children in Alaska,
the sixth – a young president somewhere,
say even in Sierra Leone,
the seventh would still shake a rattle in his pram,
and the tenth . . . the hundredth . . . the millionth . . .
For me it's not enough to be myself:

Let me be everyone
Every living creature usually has a mate,
But God was stingy with the carbon paper
and in his Paradise Publishing Corporation made a unique copy of me
But I shall muddle up all God's cards –
I shall confound God!
I shall be in a thousand copies to the end of my days,
So that the earth buzzes with me,
and computers go beserk in the world census of me.
I would like to fight on all your barricades, humanity.
– nestle against the Pyrenees
– swim across the Sahara
And take on the faith of the great brotherhood of man.
And when I die a smart-Alec Siberian François Villon,
Do not lay me in the earth of France or Italy,
But in our Russian Siberian earth, on a still green hill,
Where I first felt that I was everyone.

My Programme

If only every face possessed of beauty
Were united in one face –
If it were!
    How much then, with how much love, I'd love to kiss it,
For all, for all, for all . . .
If only every ugly face that's passed my way
Were united in one great ugly mug –
If it were!
    How I should love to sock it just that once,
For all, for all, for all . . .

SAFARI IN ULSTER

'The gates of the Safari park are invitingly open to car tourists. You are strongly advised not to open your car-windows, slow down or stop. The management cannot be held responsible if these rules are not observed.'

(From a guidebook)

1

Lions' fates are thorny like people's fates.
On the deceptive couch of Irish grass
lions recline like the most peaceful terrorists
of our time.
And the lions nonchalantly
    munch their breakfasts,
each one like a mute sandy dune,
and they wait for the cry of Africa
to summon them home.
Brother lion,
behind the wire fence you have not
    ceased to be real,
but each of your claws testing the wire
realized long ago that you are a prisoner.
Sister lioness,
by nature you are easily appeased.
Tourists don't anger you for long,
but how will you teach your cubs,
born captive, to hunt freely?
She gets up, apparently offended.
Quivering, aroused, she lashes her tail
and suddenly leaps at the car,
arching her body, becoming steel in the air.
Driver, did you tremble?
Are you afraid?
Blue-eyed girl, you are only twenty-three.
Your forebears were Irish rebels.
But now you've decided to drive –
drive on!
You, too, are inside this wire cage.
The only difference is – you're at the wheel.
Is the windscreen really that strong?
The car has stalled . . .
We and the lioness are together.
Suddenly – but wearily
and sorrowfully she leaned against it
and I felt she was even whispering.

Of course, these were not sobs or whispers,
but only the persecuted face of a woman,
only the terrible grief of animal knowledge
and her cry became a roar.
Sister lioness, how I wanted to share
our one secret moment with you –
for you are a woman and you won't betray.

2

I, too, have a growing cub.
How shall I watch over him?
What will they put into his little head?
What shall I put into it?
Here I am far away from Russia,
my snowy Africa,
but again I am tortured by the thought
of my son,
and the future of all children.
Here, both renowned and slandered,
enraged by the crackling fire,
in fenced-in glory I feel like a lion in a mousetrap.
But someone is trying to make me yelp
so I may prove my right to roar,
but that is just like making
the lions in Ireland yelp at Africa.
Photographers and clinging ladies ask me,
like a rare lion from the Siberian swamp
to bare my fangs,
just to smile a little,
but NEVER, of course, to roar at them!
Fame brings unemployment to lions' fangs.
Believe my words like a roar:
the poet is a hunter who is hunted,
but you understand this, lions,
only too well.

3

Sister lioness,
I was in Londonderry
where they would even shoot at your tails
where hands froze on the wheel at night
from uncertainty and the void.
And headlights wrenched a boy's face out of the darkness.
It was dotted with freckles
and drops of rain.

A soldier in a camouflage jacket dived out,
poking a machine-gun at us:
'Turn out yer lights' – he yelled,
'Quick!'
He grabbed our documents,
shaking with fear.
'Sorry, I thought you were terrorists.
They blind us with headlights.
So you're from Russia.'
'Yes, from Russia.'
'Why are you here?'
'I've been invited to read poetry.'
'Poetry? In Londonderry?
You must be crazy.
This is a place for grave-diggers, not poets.'
'Where're the hotels here?'
'What hotels?
All of 'em went up in smoke long ago.'
'What about restaurants?'
'Same thing. All blown up.
There's a Chinese one, though,
but the food's horrible.
Toads, worms, snakes and all that.
Can you use chop-sticks?'
'Yes, I can.'
Then I heard him whisper sadly.
'Yes, the Russians are a crazy people.'
And in the Chinese Garden Restaurant
we squeezed in somewhere against the wall,
like travellers enjoying a feast in a time of plague.
And we were frightened
not by octopus, scorpion or shark's fin,
but by the wind flapping the curtain in the window,
smashed by a blast.
At the rickety table,
around which the war went on,
invisibly,
I became drunker.
Now I felt like a Catholic, and now like a Protestant.
Fame was no longer worth anything.
For the first time in my life
I wanted to shout:
'I belong to the Russian Orthodox Church.'
But we didn't stay long.
We felt uneasy,
although we had gone to a place
where the shots sounded or seemed far away.

O Londonderry streets in the night,
like depots of darkness,
where a human fear of people
lurks in every tree,
where the apertures of houses are bricked up
against bullets in the night,
and all these bricks have been stolen
from the rubble of other houses.
Everything had been blown up:
town hall, law courts, honour,
the flag and the cross, the rampant shameful lies,
and freedom and progress.
We walked through the debris.
In the dark desert even an old man with a little dog,
cocking its leg against the remains of a Ford Capri,
looked fresh.
It was a beautiful silent night.
St Bartholomew's Night.

4

And the old man with the dog approached us,
striding as if through Dante's Inferno,
and he recited an Irish ballad for us,
which I shall retell you now:
'The Great Dane of a Protestant
only vaguely understood the meaning of God,
and the mangy mongrel bitch of a Catholic
was, poor thing, not a Catholic.
The Dane was not proud of its beauty,
the mongrel not ashamed of its looks,
and both, tugging at the leash,
fought towards each other,
as though towards freedom,
and Romeo and Juliet of Londonderry
stared at each other far apart . . .
The Catholic was killed on some wasteland,
while walking his dog in the evening.
and it howled until dawn,
appealing to everyone, even to layabouts,
but its dead master's hand stiffened
and would not let go of the leash.
And having polished his gold medals,
the Protestant took his Dane out in the morning.
And the good, simple-hearted dog
broke the leash
and tore towards that howling mongrel.

And forgetting it was a Protestant,
licked it
and howled together with it.'
The old man finished his story with a sigh:
'Atheist dogs are cleaner than us believers.
God has many faces,
and if that is so,
then God was born not among men,
but among dogs.'

5

So this is Safari in Ulster!
Sister lioness,
you're better off on your reserve,
swaying like an isle on blood.
So this is civilization,
when, shut indoors for months on end,
Irish children have to save themselves,
nestling against your stony tits.
Damned atomic Middle Ages
where it's harder for people to survive
than it is for lions,
when crosses are drawn not in chalk
but in blood.
'His faith isn't right – so button him up!'
I'm not a Protestant,
nor am I a Catholic,
but I fear the void of the future
when all the doors will have been blown out
where crosses have not yet been drawn.
But what is indifference?
It drinks and it chews –
will the age really lead to this: –
man exterminated by man –
suddenly a rare species?
Where are we heading?
What do we believe in
amidst so many senseless losses?
When humans become animals,
animals seem human.
And chewing politely,
when someone throws them titbits,
the lions turn their noses away
from foul-smelling mankind.

Belfast – Londonderry, 1975

MATERNITY FLOOR

In Shelley Road – named after Percy Bysshe –
An Anglo-Russian child has just been born,
Founder of the Lake School of Sodden Nappies.
Clean the mud off your shoes,
Stub out your cigarettes –
This is the Maternity Floor!
In a woman a mother is born
And discovers her pain to be pleasure;
A son is born,
   thus creating his father's rebirth.
Everything under the sun is reborn:
Russian snow falls whirling over Bournemouth
   transformed into English showers;
The white spots on the stems of Dunhill pipes
   change back into elephants' tusks;
Beefsteaks change back into cows,
Estuaries, long silted-up, start gushing again,
Geese, resurrected from their tins of *foie gras*,
Soar through the skies –
The policeman's redoubtable truncheon
Reverts to a resin
And falls from his fist like a tear.
London Bridge, which had been
   trundled off to the States,
Finds its way home on Concorde,
its moss-covered stonework
Travels first-class and drinks Guinness!
And all this has been achieved by our son –
Our wrinkle-faced miracle!
He is the bridge which joins you and me,
No one will ever dismantle *him*!
He's demanding the breast;
He's got the greediest appetite!
He's a tiny fragile bridge joining our two peoples!
Darling,
   give him a chance to move,
   don't wrap him up too tight!
Ah, if only all nations
   loved one another as we do!
But why are the new-born so wrinkled?
They screw up their faces in advance
At everything that's vile in the world!
In the ward where the women are in labour
The reporter is already poking about with his pen,
And jabs a political question
Between the baby and the breast.

Don't curdle the mother's milk!
I won't let you upset my son
    sucking away greedily,
Wrapped in the pages of Shakespeare and Pushkin
    as if in nappies.
Descended from Irish brigands
And oppressed Siberian peasants,
He's also wrapped in the Jolly Roger
And a sail from the tramps on Lake Baikal!
English supply ships bound for Murmansk
    so as to win a joint victory
Could have brought presents with them
If it hadn't been for the torpedoes.
He's a moist and happy little present!
But, almost as near, there are other presents:
Mr Barnes, only a day old, is screaming
As if he's already at Speakers' Corner.
And they're all utterly clean candidates
Who've never taken a bribe in their lives.
The largest Party in the world
Is the Party of Children!
Of course children can also be bribed
With sweets and ice-cream,
But the ones here haven't had a chance
    to be tempted!
I can see an Indian in the corridor
With something strange rolled-up under his arm.
Unrolled, it turns out to be a carpet.
He kneels down with a sigh,
Discarding his shoes,
And shy and alone whispers
A prayer for his son
Who was born next to mine.
And to make sure
    that neither an English nor a Russian Hiroshima
Will ever take place,
You, Earth, be my prayer-carpet
    for all children as well as for my son!
On the Maternity Floor
Rang out a triumphant cry:
The cry of an Anglo-Russian wrinkle-faced miracle
Clasped in the hands of Nurse Wilson!
And God in a white coat, concealed
Behind the pseudonym of Doctor Sid,
Lifted our son,
Naked as truth itself!
Three hundred years are the least that we need.
Oh, if only all the world's worries
Could be got rid of on the maternity floor!

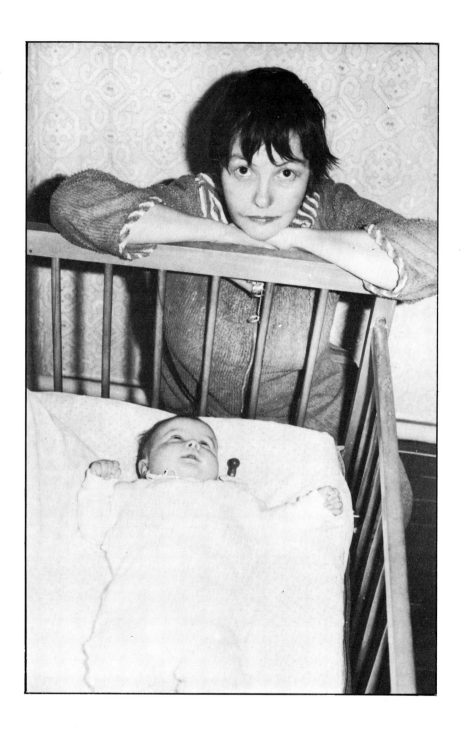

A Poet and Her Child
(Moscow)

Hard though it is to be a woman or a poet,
Being a poetess is doubly hard
For you are pregnant twice at once
– Great with child, and great with poetry.

A portrait of the greatest living Russian woman poet,
Bella Akhmadulina, with her baby

THE PHOTOGRAPHS

1 Perspective
(Malaysia)

Upon Malaysia's sandy shore there lay
A broken branch of palm
And sunset, shimmering, fell dimly gold
Upon its withered leaves.
And on the sea there rocked a boat
Whose ribs, when green, were trees;
And unseen threads, mysteriously,
Linked branch and boat as one,
As if in secret they were next of kin,
Now parted by the axe.

For me, photography, like poetry, is full of ways to overcome the distance between things. About a mile separated this branch of palm from the boat — but who knows? I find it pleasant to imagine that the boat was hewn from a tree that had been the sibling of the parent of this branch . . .

2 A Perfect Line
(Australia)

No matter what I hear of genius,
Of the great sculptors and their works,
Their Apollos and their Venuses,
Even so the marble beauty of museums
Strikes a chill.
How can such genius compare
With the sculptor who created
A live horse?

3 Kangaroo Killed by a Lorry
(Australia)

4 The Political Meeting: Detail
(Australia)

A meeting in the name of politics was under way; close by,
A body lay, so clearly unaligned
That it could hardly fail to give offence
To those who see the world divided into 'right' and 'left'.
And yet, the human person – think of it –
Is each a state, politically inclined;
And some part – say the legs – is bound to rise
Against the government, which is the head.

Photograph 4 was taken in an Australian city park, at a political meeting where moderates and extremists were engaged in some pretty uncompromising verbal sparring. To my mind though, the best statement of the day was this supine expression of the 'golden mean'.

5 Columns in the Doric Style
(Australia)

In seeing anyone who's beautiful
I'm put in mind of everyone who's not.
And think, if only beauty were the rule!
But could it, being everywhere, be seen?
And even if it could, who says it should?

6 Zima (Winter) Station
(USSR)

Here's Winter Station, in Siberia,
A witness of the only golden prize
Awarded me so far throughout my life:
In childhood days, this was – the gilded mud
Upon the surface of a stagnant pond.
Among the haughty creatures, each a swan,
That make the world of art, I recognize
Myself, a duckling from Siberia;
But I'm no farmyard creature; I'm a duck
That being wild will outfly any swan.
Over England see one feather drop to earth;
I let another fall on Patagonia.
If only I had feathers in my wings
Enough to shed one into every lake,
As a grey duckling from Siberia,
To send a message from my distant pond!

This is where I was born, in 1933. My surname, however, doesn't come from this part of the country, but from the Ukraine. Towards the end of the nineteenth century my Ukrainian peasant forebears were exiled to Siberia for rioting against their landlord. (According to family legend my great-grandmother was so strong that she killed a gendarme with a blow of her fist.) In the course of the journey, travelling on foot under police guard, they covered seven thousand kilometres.

My (hardly objective) opinion is that Siberians are the best people in Russia, Siberia having acquired so much of the country's exiled élite. Nothing unites people like shared privation; and I grew up here in an authentic atmosphere of internationalism. Russians, Ukrainians, Poles, Jews, Buryats, Chinese, and even Germans exiled here during the war, lived like next of kin. Coming from such roots has always had the effect of turning me against nationalism, or chauvinism of any kind, not least anti-semitism; and in fact the first time, uncomprehendingly, I even heard the pejorative term 'Yid' was not until 1945, after I'd left Siberia for Moscow.

In addition to its other qualities, Siberia is indescribably beautiful (if, of course, you are a voluntary visitor).

7 Alaskan Watercolour
(USA)

An Eskimo 'skidu' extends its cord
Out of Alaska's cold
To the only thing that gives off heat –
A weary human hand.
The engines that have now displaced the dogs
Weep petrol on the snow, for
When a man, exhausted, falls from cold,
They cannot lick him warm.

8 A Moscow Clown
(USSR)

9 A Woman Selling Masks
(USSR)

10 Masked Boy in New Orleans
(USA)

Some faces are like masks,
Some masks are face-like, too.
You, a Moscow circus clown;
You, boy from New Orleans;
Both of you, happy and wretched,
Tell your masks what they must do.
But can either instruct your own face?
When your mask is laughing, who knows
If the face behind is in tears?
But to make people laugh when you're crying
Is a harder thing, far nobler
Than to laugh oneself with such laughter
That others enjoy their own tears.

Pablo Neruda, in one of his last poems, wrote: 'Yevtushenko! Some people accuse you of being a clown. Congratulations on the compliment! Let us dance together on the slack tightrope strung over the sufferings of the world, giving simple joy to simple people.'

The terrible thing about being a clown is that even if you've lost a mother or a son that day you still have to go out and make people laugh. In the course of three evenings spent backstage at the circus, I took about a hundred photographs of this Russian clown. I chose photograph 8 for its suggestion of private depths far removed from any form of humour, professional or otherwise.

Photograph 9 was taken at what is known as the 'Bird Market', in Moscow; a place where you can buy things including dogs, cats, and even piglets. Standing out from the crowd was this woman selling masks which she makes herself. Strangely enough they didn't look Russian at all; they were purely African . . . invisible threads?

11, 12 Dancing on Parade
(USA/Georgia, USSR)

Dance, human beings –
But not on human bones!

13 Skyscraper and Boy
(USA)

In New York, on St Patrick's Day
Americans with Irish blood
Sat in tall buildings on the window-ledge
Like Mowglis in a jungle made of stone,
Upon the feet of kindly elephants.
An Irish boy, applauding the parade,
Made a mobile framework of his arms,
And on his shoes the laces' metal tags
Jingled arrogantly on the glass
Of my camera's peering lens.
God grant the elephants of stone
Will leave the boy uncrushed!

14 Beneath the Flags of Every Nation
(Canada)

In Canada, beneath the maple leaf
And all the other flags, from all the world,
Two blissful people stood in an embrace.
If I had my way, there would only be one flag
For all mankind, and for an emblem
There would be two people holding one another tight.

15 The Monument
(USSR)

In a Urals town, a place with industries,
Beside a monument to those who perished in the war,
A small boy stands, head bent;
And the monument, too, has bowed its head,
Longing without a doubt for just one thing –
That the war should never
Make the small boy number in its dead.

This is a monument in the Urals to the dead of the Second World War.

16 A Joiner
(Georgia, USSR)

They say a bamboo tree flowers once,
Then dies.
This bamboo died without the chance
To bloom
And you, the joiner, will translate it now
To furniture.
But what if on your tables, shoving through
The glasses, petals start to blossom forth;
And just suppose our hands are laid
Upon the table, and a tardy flower
Grows through our fingers in farewell?

17 Three Towers
(Svanetia, Georgia, USSR)

18 Their Last Easter?
(Peredelkino, USSR)

Near Moscow, at Peredelkino,
By the village church where Pasternak would go
As Easter comes, old women stand
With willow-branches, and with strong dry staffs of wood
Which once, perhaps, were willow-branches too.

19 Something Inevitable

20 The Wedding Cake
(Georgia, USSR)

Every wedding feast's a source of fear
Since domesticity,
Is often like a marriage's slow burial.

21 Before the Wedding-Feast
(Georgia, USSR)

22 Georgian Toast
(Georgia, USSR)

23 Here's to You
(Georgia, USSR)

A country wedding in Georgia is an amazing sight. Huge tarpaulin tents are erected, and at specially made tables a banquet is held for anything up to a thousand people. Guests from neighbouring villages bring cows, rams, pigs, chickens, turkeys, strong drink and fruit. In addition each guest contributes a sum of money – not less than twenty roubles – which is recorded in a special book. When there is a wedding in the donor's family, he will receive an equal or larger sum from his present hosts. Toasts are proclaimed by a master of ceremonies known as the tamadá; *the usual number of toasts is forty – with no heel-taps. Sometimes, instead of a glass, the guest is made to drain a drinking-horn which holds a third of a gallon. The only ones who do not drink are the bridal couple, who have to stand throughout. Since the wedding party lasts all night, they do sometimes pass out.*

24 A Georgian Don Juan
(Kaluga, USSR)

25 Wallflower
(Georgia, USSR)

26 A Last Tango
(Kaluga, USSR)

The young dance joyfully, as though their dance
Would have the world improve.
The old dance carefully, as though their dance
Would make the world crash down.

The dance was in a restaurant in Kaluga, a provincial city.

27 The First Steps
(Georgia, USSR)

**28 Fugitives from Their
Own Wedding**
(Siberia, USSR)

29 A Window One Might Covet
(USSR)

One window like the happiness of fairy-tales.
Beside it – what's to come.

30 Darby and Joan
(USSR)

31	**Georgian Brothers** (Georgia, USSR)	People embrace so many different ways: Friends, brothers, lovers – as all sorts.
32	**A Cuddle** (Siberia)	But even as we clasp each other we forget Death, one day, in her arms will hold us all.
33	**A Pat on the Stomach** (Georgia, USSR)	
34	**An Open Heart** (Philippines)	Too often, crossing one leg on another We hope, perhaps, to make ourselves forget
35	**You Can Trust Us!** (Philippines)	That one day we shall lie, hands crossed instead, Inside a coffin smelling of fresh wood.
36	**A Hangover** (USSR)	
37	**Siberian Threesome** (USSR)	
38	**Siberian Godfather** (USSR)	This old Siberian, seventy and more Having himself chopped every log Feels the wood's strength migrate Into himself, invincible.
39	**The Last Lama** (Buryat Republic, USSR)	In the last Buddhist temple Where quiet still reigns Amid socialism's din, This lama – is he the last? – Unwittingly appeared to me His own memorial.
40	**The Smile** (Philippines)	Gioconda is in all of us When we smile such a smile That centuries would not suffice To tell what that smile means.
41	**Radiation Sickness** (Hiroshima)	The bomb they dropped on Hiroshima, A gift from a humane society, Inside its victims every day Explodes again.
42	**A Koranic Scholar** (Malaysia)	The man who's studied the Koran No doubt has no idea That the wisest, most truthful version lies inscribed In wrinkles on his face.

48

43 With His Back to the Wall
(Malaysia)

A man with his back to the wall
In the Singapore slums.
We all have our backs to the wall
An invisible one sometimes.
But often it's we ourselves
Who build the accursed walls
Against which our fate finds us pinned
For ever.

44 Veteran and Advertisements
(USSR)

In Magadan town,
The burial-place of so many
Of Russia's best,
Exiled without a cause,
An ex-serviceman sits in the market,
A wooden hand full of cracks
Protruding from his sleeve.
Behind him are advertisements:
'Urgently wanted, for exchange, a two-room flat,
'Will pay extra for two separate rooms.'
'For sale, a second-hand bicycle going cheap.'
The crumpled advertisements rustle
Over the old man's head,
And he himself seems a want ad,
Toting at this late hour for a change of fate
Which now can't come to pass.

Taken in 1976 in the market at Magadan, a former site of hard-labour camps.
The notices advertise offers of flat-swapping, second-hand furniture, motorcycles, etc.

45 Azerbaijan Courtyard
(USSR)

46 Old Baku
(USSR)

47 In the Bosom of Christ
(USSR)

This is old Baku. In the narrow lanes
You can shake your neighbour's hand across the street
From one window to the next.
Perhaps it was a child who rendered Jesus Christ upon this
dirty wall,
And a lonely, maybe Moslem, passer-by
Has leant for consolation on the figure's breast –
In which there's an infinity of room
For all mankind's four billions and a half.

48 A Philosophical Customer
(Moscow Universal Stores)

Say what you will, a customer philosophising is one up
On a philosopher who finds himself in trade.

49 A Lost Intellectual
(Belgrade)

During the days of Tito's drawn-out death
In one quiet Belgrade street I saw
A man in a bow tie
Thoughtful-seeming, standing still as though
The old warrior's heartbeat,
Failing, could be heard.
Or was he a composer, possibly,
Listening to music of his own
As yet not written down?
Or maybe he just didn't know which way, right or left,
To turn.
Or did he stop because he sensed the passing of a life?
It is the privilege of every man
To stop and stand amid a crowd.
The crowd itself can't stop
It too is privileged – to be a crowd –
And even trample on that man
Who, perilously bold, presumes to think.

50 At Pasternak's Grave
(Peredelkino, USSR)

A girl, at Easter, came to Pasternak,
Like Lara, bearing willow-twigs.
The real Lara, now, is old
And not like Lara at all.
And this Lara too will age
And rest within the grave.
But Lara will remain eternal,
Like Easter and the budding willow-branch.
Nothing will change in her
Except her eyes, and name.

A young stranger placing the traditional Easter Day sprig of pussy willow on Pasternak's grave in Peredelkino. The site has become a place of pilgrimage for young people.

51 Philosopher and Child
(Kaluga, USSR)

Before this man, the cosmic philosopher,
A small boy stands and grins,
Pencil in hand, Tsiolkovsky halts.
What will the rocket, his invention, bring
To children everywhere?

In the Konstantin Tsiolkovsky Museum, Kaluga. Tsiolkovsky (1853–1935) was a prominent contributor to modern cosmic philosophy.

52 Yashin's Mother by the Monument to Her Son
(Nikolskoye, USSR)

The poet Alexander Yashin was a native of the village where this memorial stands. After his death the local farm-workers collected the money to build it. It is now the scene of an annual festival of poetry and song.

53 Pirosmani's Heels
(Georgia, USSR)

Pirosmani, Georgia's *Douanier* Rousseau,

Received no prizes while he was alive,

And this autumnal branch, laid here

Across his monument's bronze feet,

Is all the tribute that he has today.

Part of the monument to the Georgian painter Pirosmani, who died in poverty in 1917.

54 An Unrepentant Formalist
(Peredelkino, USSR)

The writer Viktor Shklovsky, who's survived

Two revolutions and two world wars,

Begins to look like a museum piece.

But how many objects in museums are there that

Can give you such a sly, triumphant smile?

A portrait of the writer Viktor Shklovsky, aged nearly ninety. At the time of the 1917 October Revolution, as commissar of an armoured car division for the Provisional Government, he took his division over to the side of the Bolsheviks. Among White émigré circles it was jokingly rumoured that he was the only reason why the Bolsheviks won. He was close to Mayakovsky, and wrote literary essays for which he was strongly criticized as a 'formalist'. He refused to yield one inch to his critics, however; and supported Mandelstam when the latter was in disgrace. He is still as stubborn as ever.

55 Chance Encounter
(Paris)

In Paris, by a newspaper kiosk, I had an unexpected encounter with Comrade Stalin. Perhaps this bystander also had him in his thoughts.

56 Right Behind Lenin
(Georgia, USSR)

For people who are symbols now,

Their greatness is the vantage-point from which we're seen.

Most people will be no such thing,

Yet say who will that their humanity will cease.

57 Lenin
(Tbilisi, USSR)

Giant plyboard portrait of Lenin, covering the whole wall of a building. It was put up during the celebrations for the anniversary of the October Revolution. The open door leads into a hall where a banquet has been prepared for the government and special guests.

58 The Price of Greatness
(Moscow)

Taken in GUM, Moscow's largest store. On sale are little sculptures of Lenin as a child, the poet Pushkin, and Felix Dzerzhinsky – the founder of the CHEKA.

59 Sweet Smiles from the Chief Prospector's Bodyguards
(Siberia)

Of all anthologies the first and best

Is found in human faces.

60 An Unclear Horizon
(Moscow)

61 The Chief Prospector
(Siberia)

Formerly, this man was navigator on a ship in the Pacific. He was arrested and convicted of 'subversive activity' for having recited from the poetry of Yesenin, which until the Second World War was suppressed. He made several escapes, but each time he was caught. Having been sentenced to life – seventy years' – imprisonment, he worked in various labour camps as a gold-miner. It was found he had such a good nose for nuggets that it was agreed to count each year of his sentence as seven, and after ten years he was released. He resurrected a private prospectors' cooperative in the Siberian forest, consisting mostly of former inmates of the camps, and he now commands five hundred people, using the best Soviet helicopters, Japanese excavators and American caterpillars. They produce about three tons of gold a year. Probably his is the only gold-mining company where nobody steals; the average monthly wage is 1,500 roubles – ten times the national average wage and twice the salary of the Soviet Prime Minister. A brilliant man. He doesn't write poetry, but he still loves it.

62 The Georgian
(Siberia)

63 The Big Boss's Driver
(USSR)

64, 65 Men of Affairs
(Australia/Georgia, USSR)

Business folk in Melbourne or Sukhumi
Look down upon us poets with an air
That seems to say their wallets hold
The secrets of the world.
But once, when someone asked me
Of a banker,
'Isn't he a very clever man?'
I answered, having thought, and said
'A clever man? Like Shakespeare?'

(One photograph is of businessmen at the Melbourne races; the other shows well-to-do Georgians who have come to Sukhumi for a wedding.)

66 He Killed his Wife
(Siberia)

This man has been sentenced many times, for various kinds of robbery. After an escape from prison, at the age of sixty, he discovered his wife (also sixty) with another man. He killed her with a flat-iron, the result being another prison sentence. Eventually he was released on account of his age. He's now about eighty years old. He told me a marvellous story: once, after his gang had stolen two thousand pairs of woollen gloves from a store, they were accused at their trial of having stolen leather gloves. This version was of course much more profitable for the director of the store. The old man's comment was: 'How can men with morals like that exist in a socialist society?'

67 Allied with a Shovel
(Georgia, USSR)

Smiling, the workers of the world
Can do enough and more
To light up all the world at once.
And when they're sad
Their melancholy is a force
Mighty enough to blow up every cause
That lies beneath their suffering.

68 The Bricklayer
(USSR)

69 Toothache
(Baku, USSR)

70 Tipping a Wink
(Siberia)

71 Reflection
(USSR)

72 La Pasionaria
(Spain)

Dolores Ibarruri has grown old
Since she was known among the Spanish people
Fighting in defence of their Republic
As 'La Pasionaria'.
Her son died at Stalingrad
And, back at last in Spain,
She's like a Joan of Arc who's fled the fire,
And at times, perhaps, regrets
That after all she didn't perish at the stake.

A portrait of Dolores Ibarruri, known as the 'Joan of Arc' of the Spanish Civil War. She lived in the Soviet Union from 1937, returning to Spain after Franco's death. I took this photograph at a congress in support of Chilean democrats, in 1978.

73 The Shadow of Gravity
(USSR)

74 A Siberian Vendor of Chewing Gum
(USSR)

Siberian peasants brew chewing gum from resin.

75 Take Your Pick!
(Siberia)

76 Grandmother
(USSR)

To tell the truth I never much admire
The beauty of the elegance in mannequins.
All women, in their way are beautiful
And, likewise, ugliness itself.
And even age is beautiful, did it but know.

82 Classical Australia
(Australia)

What, now, do you think of, cart,
At your creaking journey's end?
Parting, creak a message out,
Across the racket of the atom age!

83 The Colosseum
(Rome)

All empires are like dinosaurs,
Their giant size spells doom.
Coca Cola is the only one
That merrily expands.
And yet I know that empire too
Will someday meet its end.

84 Where Pasolini Died
(Rome)

Pasolini took me to the slums of Rome several times. He had a strangely masochistic attraction to poverty and cruelty. Despite his greatness as a poet, like many of his kind in the West he found it impossible to make enough to live on just by writing poetry. So his search for a means of public confession led him instead to cinema. When in 1963 I came under strong government criticism I was surprised to receive from him a two-page telegram of congratulation. 'I envy you,' it said; 'here in Italy I could take off all my clothes, climb into the fountain on the Piazza di Espagnia and recite anything I liked, and nobody would take any notice.' After Pasolini offered me the part of Christ in his film The Gospel According to St Matthew *Khrushchev received a letter signed by several Italian intellectuals, including Alberto Moravia and Vittorio di Sica, assuring him that Pasolini's film would interpret Jesus Christ from a strictly Marxist point of view – but it made no difference.*

85 Russian Mother
(USSR)

I must be honest with you: this is my own mother. Back in the twenties she was very left-wing. This meant of course that she was also a militant atheist – so to have me baptized, my grandmother had to take me off to church in secret. My parents both studied at the Geological Institute, during which time my father was expelled from the Young Communists. His offence was wearing a tie, a form of behaviour which was considered a bourgeois superstition.

(Strangely enough, during the seventies, not long before his death, he was refused admission to a Moscow restaurant for not wearing one.) As a young man my father was a poet of some talent. Paradoxically, though, he spent his whole working life in the world of technology; whereas my mother, for whom poetry meant little, came to spend much of her life as an artist. When, suddenly, she was found to have a good singing voice, she gave up working as a geologist and became an operetta singer. During the war she toured the front, singing, even in snowstorms, in trenches and dug-outs and on the backs of lorries. Sometimes she gave up to twenty concerts a day. Eventually, it ruined her voice; and she turned to organizing concerts for children, and stretching her small salary to bring me up (my parents were divorced by then). When she came to retire, she did not know what to do with herself: she had worked all her life. So she took a job selling newspapers. She is the only person I am afraid of (and justly so!). All my poetry is the child of her lost voice.

86 The Smile of Asia
(Manila)

In Manila, smiling, this fisherman has no idea
He is the subject of *The Old Man and the Sea*
– And yet is not.
Meanwhile the sea itself makes up a book
That nobody has read through to the end.

87 A Look of Surprise
(Philippines)

Surprising others is a knack that some
Can even practise as professionals,
Though, tragically, beyond surprise themselves.
And who's the happier man? Why, he's the one
Surprised.

88 Kobo Abe
(Japan)

The writer Kobo Abe from Japan,
A leader in his craft.
You'll see him look compassion; and although
Rogues suffer too, I know
The woes of others only touch a few.

There are a number of modern writers who make me want to read every word they've ever written: among them, Gabriel García Marquez, Heinrich Böll, William Golding – and the Japanese novelist Kobo Abe (who, in addition to being a writer, is also a wonderful photographer).

89 A Craftsman's Hands
(Australia)

Human hands resemble manuscripts
That, being written in a language that's extinct,
No one can read.

The hands of Australian enameller, Ninette Dutton.

90 Doing the Wash
(USSR)

At Vologda, here in Russia's northern heart,
A washerwoman kneels.
Across the river from her stands a church.
One might think she prays,
And the church, seeing her work as well, forgives,
Because another woman,
Painted on icons with the Christ Child in her arms,
Once used to wash his swaddling-clothes.

91 Pearl-divers
(Japan)

Japanese women in masks
Dive for pearls,
But who will dive
For these women
Who do not know
That they are pearls themselves?

92 Transparency
(Philippines)

A Filipino boy stands in a sea
So clear that in it he can view
The toes upon his hesitating feet,
Driftwood, and broken bits of net
So sodden that the water weighs far less.
Be careful, child! For you may step
Upon a rusty nail concealed by sand.
You cannot trust in that transparency!
For nothing in the world will show that clear.

93 Siberian 'Deliverance'
(USSR)

Together with friends, I have so far travelled, by boat and raft, down five of Siberia's fiercest rivers. This is the artist Oleg Tselkov, on the Vilyuy River, which carried us two thousand kilometres. It is very difficult to obtain detailed maps of Siberia, since they are all classified as secret. When one of us did get hold of some, they showed about fifty rapids on the Vilyuy – but when we came to travel down them we were surprised to find they really numbered more than a hundred. By the end of the journey we had ruined two motors colliding with rocks, and we limped home with a third bent out of all recognition: we had to replace one of the bolts with a piece of stick. We came to the conclusion that the best way to fool the Pentagon would be to give them a presentation set of our classified maps. After the trip I wrote:

Some clot, completely assified
Declared our maps all 'classified'.
First they drew them full of lies,
Then they say 'not for *your* eyes!'

56

94 The Drunken Cow
(Japan)

The cow
        lamented
                sobbing violently,
Swaying like a drunkard.
Her coat was black
Like the black smoke of Hiroshima.
Her groans shook
The gloomy cow temple.
Her seven hundred kilos
Made the earth sag.
People are sensitive,
However,
           only
Before the nice warm beef
Has reached the plate.

While in Japan I was offered a local beef fondue known as suki-yaki. *My hosts explained that one reason why it was juicy and tender was that the cows are fed on beer. I thought they were joking. The Japanese do not care not to be taken seriously; and next day they took me to a slaughterhouse, where I saw what you see in the photograph.*

95 Portrait from Samarkand
(Uzbekistan, USSR)

All the beauty in the world
Is only fit to be a frame for womankind.

96 At Tamerlane's Tomb, in Samarkand
(Uzbekistan, USSR)

When archaeologists, in 1941,
Prepared to open Tamerlane's sarcophagus
In the Uzbek city of Samarkand,
A crowd collected round the monument.
People waved their hands and shouted:
'Don't touch it! A great spirit of war
Will burst forth from the grave!'
But the archaeologists paid no attention
To these dire forebodings.
They opened the sarcophagus,
And a cloud of black smoke billowed out.
There was a scientific explanation – they were pent-up gases,
But on the very next day war broke out.
You, little boy, sucking your lollipop
In front of Tamerlane's sarcophagus,
Don't get too close,
Or touch the marble lid
On the tomb where, maybe, the war-god lies asleep.

I took the photograph of the tomb of Tamerlane in Samarkand from the gallery above. It was very dark, and although I had a 400 ASA film I had to open the aperture to 15. This little boy was standing alone by the tomb, and looked up at me just at the very last moment. I was sure it would spoil the picture; but as it turned out I think it was the making of it.

97 Early Snow
(USSR)

I'd left some flowers out on the balcony,
And, unexpectedly, that night it snowed.
Through the basket handle thick with snow,
Like a rainbow made of grey,
I looked, and saw that in the garden,
Autumn had changed for winter in the night.
So it is with human beings, too
Who, quite surprisingly, age overnight.
But still we hope the winter of our lives
Will turn again to spring.

One day towards the end of September I put out this basket of pansies on the balcony of my dacha outside Moscow. Subsequently when I opened the door one early morning I was surprised to find them covered in snow.

98 A Cold-War Hero
(Moscow)

99 A Cold-War Heroine
(Moscow)

An engineer, maybe he's director of a trust,
Has pierced the ice to angle after fish,
Although at home – no bother – he can have black caviar.
A woman, too, an English grammar by her side,
Bends patiently above the punctured ice.
Below, the little fishes look at them,
And maybe even bite from time to time,
From pity for the humans in the cold.

A common Russian hobby in winter is fishing through the ice with a short line. The drill pierces the ice. The fishermen stay out all day, and when I took photograph 98 it was −40°F. When asked 'Aren't you cold?' the man replied, 'Nothing like a healthy frost to kill off any germs.'

An exceptional sight: a women fishing through the ice in an expensive astrakhan coat with a polar-fox collar. When I asked her what the book was she replied 'Advanced English'.

100 On Lake Baikal
(Siberia)

On Lake Baikal this young fisherman
Pulls in his net, and maybe every fish
Whispers inaudibly
In words he'll never truly understand;
But if he did
He'd never be a fisherman again.

101 First Violets
(Tbilisi, Georgia)

102 Cigar and Roses
(Philippines)

An old man at Tbilisi, selling violets,
Their petals thick with snow;
A woman from the Philippines with heavy hands,
Her roses no more weighty than the smoke
From that cigar between her teeth –
Though knowing nothing of each other, they are
kinsfolk through their flowers;
And in all their trade there's no one I despise,
Unless their goods are plunder from fresh graves.

103 Weighed down in Red Square
(Moscow)

104 Captive Shopper
(Moscow)

105 A Broken Heel
(Moscow)

In Moscow a provincial visitor,
Arms weighted by her purchases,
Shows how a specially female gravity
Draws bags and cases down.
Another woman, sitting on the things she's bought,
Imprisoned in a store.
A woman by a mausoleum,
With a shoe whose heel is wrong,
And whose bag, beside her, rests,
Itself a small but ponderous mausoleum,
The grave of her lost youth.

106 A Victim of Gossip
(USSR)

Everybody in this village in Siberia
Stares at this woman, of whom someone said,
Once, 'She's a tramp.'
And so the label stuck,
And no one knows that it's untrue,
That over twenty years she's slept alone
With her knees cold against the chilly wall.

107 Her Rival the Bottle
(Lithuania, USSR)

108 The Arbour
(France)

Madame Hélène Martini, *patronne* of the Folies Bergère,
Schéhérazade, Raspoutine and who knows how many bars,
Herself will only drink a glass of vodka every while.
Behind her elegant back there always runs barbed wire,
        from Stalin's camps.
While here she is, depicted in the country, at her home
Within an arbour overgrown with ivy, in an iron cage.

109 In the Same Cage
(Moscow)

In the Moscow market the man with doves for sale
Must have fought in World War Two,
And now to all appearances he's caged
With the birds so sentimentally called doves of peace.

110 Marcello Mastroianni
(Italy)

I hardly ever photograph celebrities,
And if I do then only when
Their fame is something they've just overlooked.

Taken in 1979, during an interval in the making of Fellini's film La Città
delle Donne.

111 His Last Cigarette
(Buryat Republic, USSR)

*This is a portrait of the Buryat writer Batojapai. He was formerly a horse-
herdsman , and a powerful giant of a man. We were student friends – though
I never saw him at lectures, because he was always too busy enjoying life in
other ways. When I saw him for the last time he was dying of cancer, and had
lost thirty kilos. People had tried to hide the truth from him, but he'd guessed
all the same. He asked me for a cigarette, and when I looked enquiringly at his
wife he said: 'Don't worry. Give me a cigarette; it will be my last. Take my
picture – my last picture, too.' The next day he died.*

112 Taking the Trick
(USSR)

The Moscow lawyer playing 'preference'
Has failed to realize that he is himself a card
Or that the hand that holds him is invisible.

113 Artistic Cunning
(USSR)

Moscow artist, I will help you
Show the thing you've overlooked –
Your own face.

114 Futurology
(Paris)

Here again is Oleg Tselkov,
A constant hero in my photographs,
At the *Salon d'automne*, perplexedly scratching his head
At figures who've no backs to theirs.

115 Two Women
(USSR)

At a Moscow exhibition, silently,
A woman writes a review
And stops to think, beneath a picture
That's thinking, sadly, of her.

116 Vigilance
(USSR)

In a small Siberian town,
Near the clinic where I was born,
This man looked at me
With such suspicion that I
Might have been born commissioned
By a secret organization
To recruit everyone in the world.

117 Old and Young
(England)

118 Piccadilly
(London)

In Piccadilly Circus a hippy
Reclines on the steps –
Unable to make an ascent.

119 Trafalgar Square
(London)

I hope the pigeon perched on this girl's head
Is not a hawk, disguised.

120 A Dying Swan
(London)

Weary and varicose-veined, a dying swan;

121 A Beggar
(London)

A begging dwarf;
An old man dancing for coppers –
These are my poor brethren in Christ;

122 A Money-Spinner
(London)

Myself, Toulouse-Lautrec of Leicester Square.

123 His Final Argument
(London)

I love Hyde Park; the saddest exhibitions
Of would-be liberty can happen here –

124 A Kind of Trampoline
(London

Freedom that was not, is not, and can't be;
For our illusions lie too deep in each of us.

125 Cheerleader
(Moscow)

Professional good-mood-maker in a Moscow park. She sings the verses of the song, and holds up the words of the chorus so that the audience can join in. In spite of all her enthusiasm, though, nothing can hide the fact that the words of such songs are usually bland to the point of mindlessness. The ones in the picture read:
      'Sun shining in the sky?
      Marvellous, just marvellous'.
      Snow falling everywhere?
      Marvellous, just marvellous.'

126 A Fragile Pedestal
(London)

127 Hyde Park Corner
(Siberia, USSR)

128 An Admonitory Finger
(London)

In the background is the maternity ward where I was born. Because of my Nikon, this man suspected me of being an American spy, and launched into an impassioned speech for peace.

129 Thrown Together
(Moscow)

Every bench a little island
Of despair and hope.

130 A Political Lecture
(Moscow)

At a lecture on international affairs
People doubtless forget
That international relations are themselves.

131 Self-discovery
(Australia)

Beside the loss of self how much more scary
It can be to suffer self-discovery.

This was taken at a race meeting in Australia. I had two prints from the same negative; and by chance I saw them lying side by side. Their coincidence suddenly struck me as creating an appealing, rather melancholy effect, so I made them into one picture.

132 In Hyde Park
(London)

133 A Public Nap
(Australia)

134 A Philosopher
(Siberia)

The earth no doubt assists
The weary who lie down on it
But who in turn will help the earth?
Where will it lay itself to rest?

135 Alms
(USSR)

136 Counting Coins
(Moscow)

I speak for everyone who counts loose change
But not for those whose millions are so many
They cannot even count them in their heads.

**137 Newton: a Victim of
Gravity Again**
(London)

Monument to Isaac Newton, pictured during the dustmens' strike of 1979.

138 The Olympian
(London)

Arthur Boyars, as an intellectual a member of a dying race
Chose the background for this photograph himself –
Or did the background pick on him?

139 Madrid Townscape
(Spain)

For me, this puppet, lying in a street in Madrid, gave a strange impersonation of a living person surrounded by rubbish yet trying to survive.

140 The Cleaner and the Monument
(Lithuania, USSR)

A woman with a mop, cleaning the pedestal
Of a famous general's monument
Does not realize her own worth
Exceeds the world's whole sum of pedestals.

141 A Backward Look
(Moscow)

Little boy on Moscow's Red Square
Behind me, what's there to see?
Tell me what colour your horizon is.

142 Cut-price Transport
(New York)

People shouldering people, there's no doubt,
Are less extraordinarily rare
Than people helping people.

143 Poverty and Grace
(Philippines)

You know which party has the greatest membership?
– The party of the child.

144 They Love Photographers
(Philippines)

145 Fear or Curiosity?
(Singapore)

146 Distrust
(Philippines)

147 High Jinks
(Philippines)

148 At the Circus
(Moscow)

**149 Behind the Scenes
at the Circus**
(Moscow)

An acrobat reclines against her mirrored self –
Or does the image lean on her?

150 The Horse-trainer
(Moscow)

A man who trains the horses at the Moscow circus has a face
To suit a Dostoyevskian protagonist.

151 A Japanese Lolita
(Japan)

Lolita, Australian or Japanese,
Is really Bluebeard

152 The Temptress
(Australia)

Posing as a girl.

153 Two Puerto Rican Boys
(New York)

Seated here, how beautifully they sing,
Upon such ugly news.

154 Children at UNESCO
(Paris)

At UNESCO, at a session where the children were
Delegated to receive their elders –
Busy, these latter, saying childish things –
A bull-faced boy, just like Napoleon,
Chanced to find himself behind the plate whose title read:
Director-General.

Children at UNESCO assembled to welcome guests to the building. By chance one of the boys found himself behind the label 'Directeur Général'.

**155 A London Anne Frank
in the Underground**
(England)

In the London tube a Jewish girl,
Hemmed in by passengers on every side,
Looked like Anne Frank who'd suddenly observed
Gestapo, in the carriage corner, in disguise.

156 A Difference of Style
(England)

You'll have no trouble guessing which
Of these two women –
Women both of them, but how unlike! –
Made me fall in love.

157 My Russia
(Siberia)

My Russia isn't monuments or slogans,
But, like my conscience gazing at me silently, this little girl.

2

3

4

6

9

10

13

14

15

20

21

22

23

24

25

28

34

36

37

38

40

42

43

46

47

48

50

51

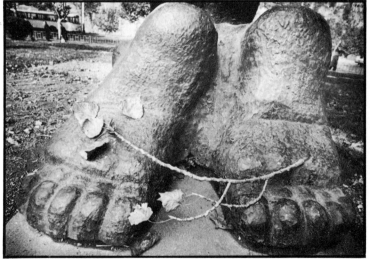

56

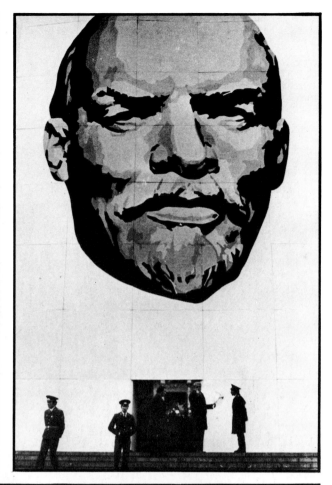

57

58

59

60

62

61

63

64

67

68

69

70

71

72

76

77

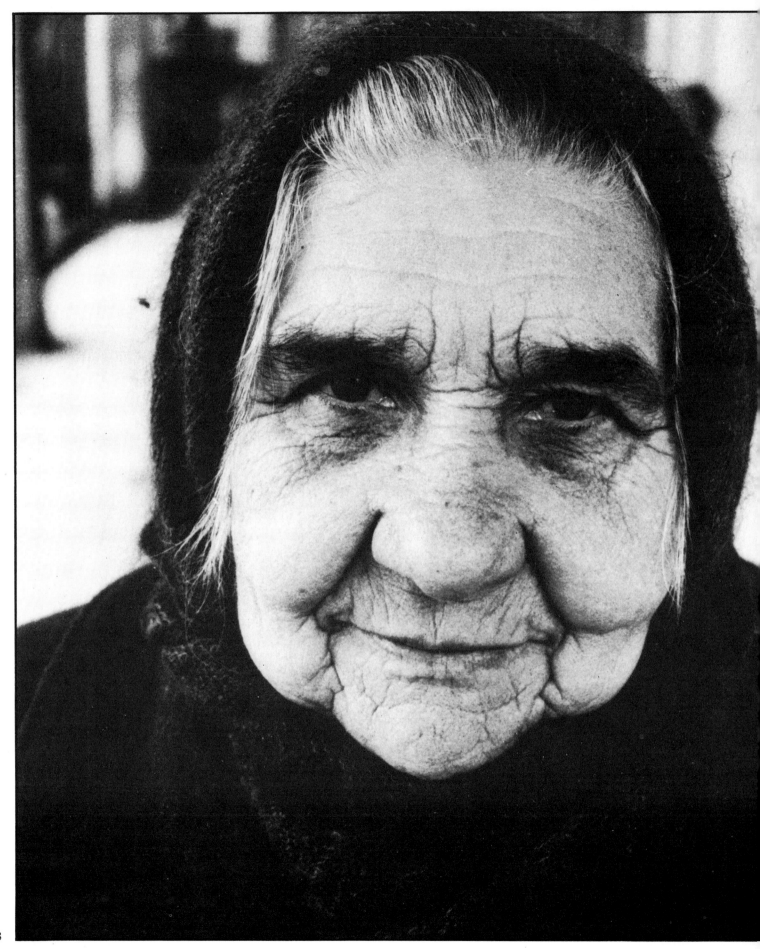

83

84

86

87

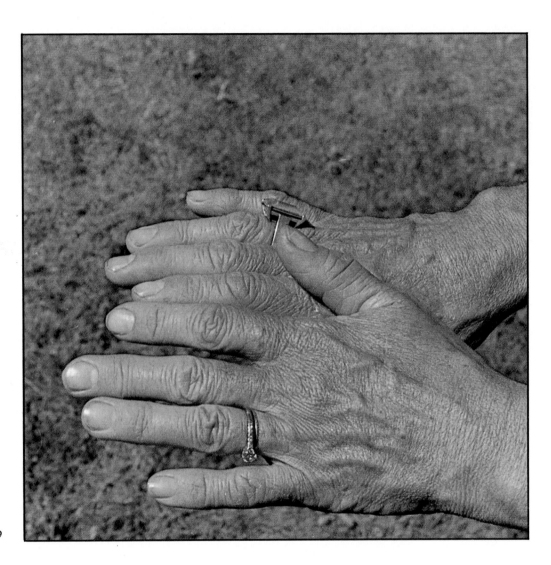

94

96

97

107

109

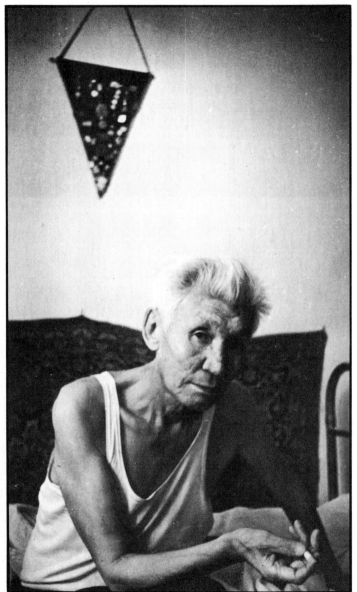

114

115

121

122

125

126

127

128

133

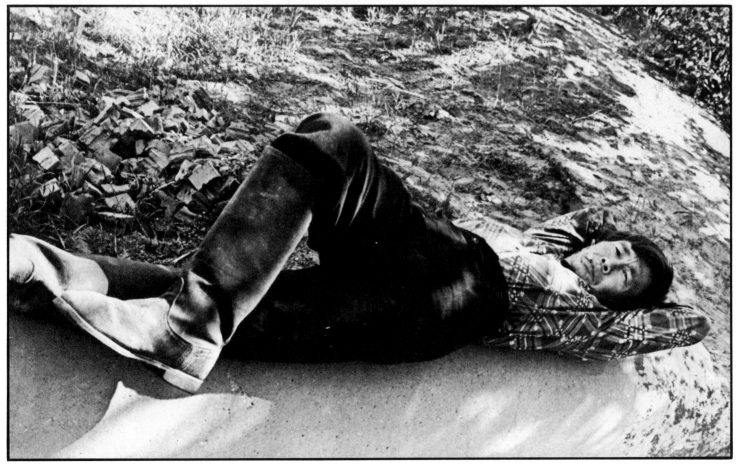

134

138

139

140

141

142

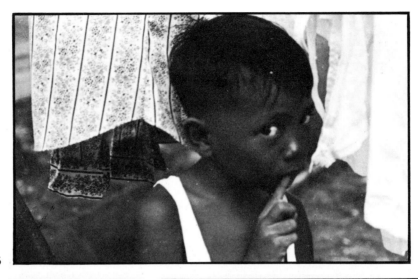

145

146

147

148

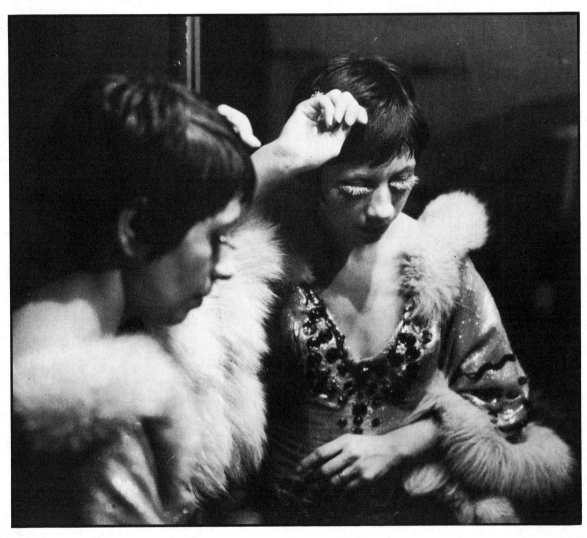

149

151

152

DIRECTEUR GENERAL

155

156